HOW TO

FREEZE YOUR BIOLOGICAL CLOCK

Unlock Your Freedom

HOW TO

FREEZE YOUR BIOLOGICAL CLOCK

Unlock Your Freedom

The essence of this book is to empower the young Millennials and Gen Z of society, so they can prioritize work-life balance and purpose in their lives.

EMPOWERED WOMAN = POWERFUL SOCIETY

DR. Gunjan Gupta

International Fertility and IVF Expert

PENDOWN PRESS LLP

An ISO 9001 & ISO 14001 Certified Co.,

Regd. Office: 3767A, Kanhaiya Nagar,
Tri Nagar, Delhi-110035
Ph.: 8130886000, 9650072927
E-mail: info@pendownpress.com
Branch Office: 1A/2A, 20, Hari Sadan, Ansari Road,
Daryaganj, New Delhi-110002
Ph.: 011-45794768
Website: PendownPress.com

Edition: 2025
Price: ₹ 449/-
ISBN: 978-93-5554-989-1

Layout and Cover Designed by Pendown Graphics Team
Printed and Bound in India by Thomson Press India Ltd.

- *Dedicated to my parents who taught me to dream.*
- *To my husband Pradyot, daughter Samriddhi, my entire family, mentors, and friends who cheered me on, And*
- *My patients who bring these pages to life.*

CONTENTS

Foreword

Dr. USHA SHARMA
Padmashri Awardee
MBBS, MS (Obs & Gyn), Dip. in Infertility (U.S.A.)

Ex. – Director General Medical Education, Uttar Pradesh
–Principal-cum-Professor of Gynaecology & Obstetrics, LLRM Medical College, Meerut
–Dean Faculty of Medicine, Ch. Charan Singh University, Meerut
Chief Patron of U.P. chapter of Obst. & Gynecology

FOREWORD

"Helping one person might not change the whole world, but it could change the world for one person"

Women's healthcare which has gained importance recently is an important subject, most certainly with regards to fertility. The technique of fertility preservation through egg freezing is a monumental breakthrough.

Penning the foreword for Dr. Gunjan Gupta Govil's, "How to Freeze Your Biological Clock Unlock Your Freedom" fills me with great hope and delight, as it is set to be a transformative guide for women navigating through the delicate balance between career aspirations and the desire for motherhood.

With decades of experience, I have witnessed firsthand the challenges women face due to infertility, miscarriages, being busy growing their career in their 20s, and not being able to bear children later due to low fertility. The societal pressures, the ticking biological clock, and unforeseen health issues can often create a daunting path to choosing motherhood and then enjoying it fully. Egg freezing has been a term in books since the 1980s, but it has never actually been used in practice very frequently. Seeing this noble thought being materialised in front of me gives me immense happiness, and I applaud Dr. Gunjan for sensitising many people about this.

With the growing incidence of diseases like Endometriosis, premature ovarian failure, etc., and also the deadly impact of environmental pollutants that decrease the ovarian reserve quite early, some females lose their eggs as early as the age of 30. Cryopreservation provides a ray of hope for these females to have their own biological child.

“Motherhood is a choice you make every day to put someone else’s happiness and well-being ahead of your own”. Hence this a choice a woman should make on her own terms. Whether it is to achieve career goals, wait for the right partner, or simply to have peace of mind, the insights and guidance offered here will empower women to make informed decisions about their reproductive health. She authentically addresses every aspect making this book an invaluable resource for women who are about to undergo this journey.

Priyanka Chopra's decision to freeze her eggs, as highlighted in the preface, is a powerful testament to the liberation and peace of mind that comes with this choice. Through the compelling stories of the women who have embarked on this journey of fertility preservation, Dr. Gunjan through the book paints a vivid picture of the potential life-changing impact of egg freezing.

It is rightly said that,
“ Finding a good doctor is like finding a long lost friend, with whom you can share everything and half the cure is their words.”

"How to Freeze Your Biological Clock Unlock Your Freedom" is more than a book about freezing eggs; it is about freezing freedom— the freedom to dream, to aspire, and to choose motherhood on one's own terms.

Dr. Gunjan’s mission to educate and support women through this book resonates with my lifelong commitment to advancing women's health and well-being. I as principal of a medical college for 20 years and DGME (Director General Medical Education) for the state of Uttar Pradesh have seen the sad plight of women in the most populous state of Uttar Pradesh. Along with helping patients, I myself have always tried to educate the gynaecologists and masses about new prospectus in gynaecology.

I wish Dr. Gunjan Gupta Govil massive success not only for this book but also in her venture of providing new hope to women in the future and making egg freezing a procedure accessible and known to all.

USHA SHARMA
Chief Patron
UPCOG

Preface

Freeze Your Freedom: Create An Open Window of Opportunity

Now, that's Priyanka Chopra who chose the path of freedom by freezing her eggs so that she could pursue her career as well as wait for the right person to have children with, **without her biological clock holding a gun to her head every single passing month and year.**

On the other hand, as you will see further in the book, **there are women who have lost their reproductive ability due to various unforeseen reasons and wish somebody had told them about the option of freezing their eggs instead of facing life with unfulfilled dreams & longings.**

While motherhood is a choice that every woman should be allowed to exercise at her will, for those who wish to become biological mothers, the inability to do so can be an unimaginable pain.

As a woman how many times have you heard these questions:

- **Kaam pe hi dhyaan deti rahogi to maa kab banogi, umer aur waqt tumhaare liye nahin rukenge!**

  [If you keep focusing on work, when will you become a mother? Age & time are not going to wait for you!]

- **Shaadi ki bhi ek umer hoti hai, jab bachche paida karne**

me dikkat aayegi toh humein mat kehna!

[There is a right time to get married, later if you face problems getting pregnant don't blame us]

- **Ab tum bachcha toh de nahin sakti, humaare kis kaam ki?**

  Now that you cannot bear a child, what use are you to us?

I promise you I will come back to these questions later, right now I want to share 3 real-life stories with you (names changed for privacy) briefly, later in the book I will share these with you in detail except for Neha's story that I am sharing below.

It is because of these pressures, fears and frustration that the concept of social egg-freezing came to the rescue of women wanting more out of life.

Social egg preservation, also known as elective or non-medical egg freezing, involves the extraction, cryopreservation, and **storage of a woman's eggs with the aim of protecting her fertility for future non-medical reasons** [as the above example of Priyanka Chopra demonstrates].

Originally, egg-freezing technology was developed to help women undergoing medical treatments, such as chemotherapy or radiation therapy, that could harm their fertility. **However, social egg-freezing has gained popularity among women who wish to delay childbearing for personal or professional reasons.**

Several factors influence the decision to undergo social egg-freezing, including career goals, educational pursuits, financial stability, relationship status, and personal preferences.

Women who choose social egg-freezing see it as a means

to take control of their reproductive future and maintain the option of having genetically related children later in life when they feel more ready or secure in their circumstances.

Advancements in egg-freezing technology and a better understanding of fertility preservation have contributed to the growing acceptance and prevalence of social egg-freezing.

Neha's Lost Opportunities & Health

Shining Bright

Neha was a bright student right from childhood, great at academics as well as co-curricular activities. Everyone believed she would be a shining light in the corporate world once she joined a reputed MNC after she passed her MBA with flying colours.

She kept climbing up the corporate ladder speedily and smoothly. She also met her soulmate at her office and soon they got married.

Life was great, they were the exemplary power couple, the darlings of the office until Neha became pregnant one fine (or not so fine) day due to a contraceptive failure.

A Twist in The Tale

When the news was confirmed everybody except Neha was overjoyed, Neha wasn't mentally prepared to be a mother yet, she wanted a few more years to focus on her career so that when she became a mother, she would be ready to welcome the little one wholeheartedly.

She contemplated terminating the pregnancy but everyone around her kept reminding her that she was 31 already and getting no younger and this was the right time, this was a God-sent opportunity and a signal from the universe. Such was the pressure on her that she agreed to carry the pregnancy through.

However, Neha couldn't enjoy the first stage of this beautiful journey to motherhood as her mind wouldn't allow her to be fully present to the joys of carrying a new life, this stressed her both physically & mentally causing complications in her pregnancy leading to complete bed rest.

Struggling to Find the Self

Neha had to take a long leave from her work, right when she was due for a promotion and to lead a project that she had wanted for long. All her hard work went down the drain.

This took a toll on Neha, confined to her bed, her mind worked like the enemy to remind her of what she had lost and her mental health took a hit, especially as her husband who worked in the same organization was effortlessly climbing all the rungs that she too deserved to climb. Things didn't improve much after she gave birth to the baby. She went into post-partum depression.

To cut a long story short, Neha had to take 3 years off work and in those 3 years she couldn't even be fully present with her baby and experience the joys & challenges of motherhood. Those were the hardest 3 years of her life when they could have been the happiest.

Neha did go back to work and became involved with her child, building a great bond, however, the trauma she went through could so easily have been prevented.

Had somebody told Neha about the option of freezing her eggs, this story could have been written very differently saving so much pain, struggle, tears & time.

Unlocking the potential of egg freezing can revolutionize your life as a woman (and as a couple), transcending age, profession, career stage, disease, health, etc.

This book is a condensation of my two decades+ of experience in empowering individuals to choose & embrace their fertility journey, at their own pace & in their own time I bring a wealth of knowledge and passion to this conversation & choice.

More importantly, not just my passion & profession, giving women the gift of time & freedom is my mission.

The reason I am writing this book is so that women never have to choose between fulfilling the choices of life versus becoming a mother.

I can help women preserve their fertility enabling them to become mothers exactly when they choose to and not because they are sitting on the ticking time bomb of their biological clock & age.

Trust me, I speak from my expertise in delivering Khushiyon ki Goonj.

Greetings, I am Dr. Gunjan Gupta Govil.

I am humbled that I am often referred to as a trailblazer in the realm of fertility and IVF by both my peers and my patients.

My immersion into the world of egg freezing came about a decade ago when I began witnessing its adoption by celebrities and Icons to choose a life of freedom to navigate their professional trajectories as well as become parents when they felt that they were completely (read emotionally, financially, physically & mentally) ready to embrace parenthood wholeheartedly.

Since then, my journey into preserving fertility has continually reaffirmed my belief in its ability to empower women (and couples) with autonomy and freedom.

My mission is to enlighten, empower and embolden women across diverse spheres with the transformative potential of egg freezing.

Through careful & detailed guidance and unwavering support, my team & I have facilitated countless clients in navigating fertility preservation effortlessly.

Whether driven by career aspirations, educational pursuits, financial considerations, or health adversities like suffering from cancer, our clients have embarked on the path to parenthood with confidence and grace and most importantly on their own terms and timings.

At this point, I am sure many of you would be wondering why I am offering this e-book for free when its insights could command a premium.

The answer is simple!

My motivation stems from my commitment to making fertility education and support accessible to every woman in India.

I want every woman to know that she has the option to beat the biological clock by freezing her eggs.

I want all women to know that they never have to choose between this or that simply because age is running out on them and they have to hurry up and embrace motherhood, else this joy will pass them by.

However, due to the constraints of time and logistics, it is impossible for me to reach and support everyone personally. That is where this book comes in, this e-book is meant to serve as a guiding light for women grappling with the intricacies of infertility and work-life balance.

So, let's set out on this journey together, discovering the endless possibilities that egg freezing brings. As your trusted fertility guide, I pledge my unwavering dedication to guiding you towards a future of chosen parenthood overflowing with joy and fulfilment.

Joyfully Yours,

Dr. Gunjan Gupta Govil
Your Fertility Expert

Acknowledgements

Firstly, I would like to express my heartfelt gratitude to my husband, Dr. Pradyot Govil, whose unwavering support has empowered me to achieve more than I ever dreamed possible.

I also owe a special thanks to my daughter, Samriddhi, whose encouragement prompted me to reflect on the challenges young women face today in balancing work and life. Her insights have deepened my commitment to empowering them.

I am deeply grateful to my team at Gunjan IVF World, especially Mr. Gurav Singhai, Dr. Aastha Raheja, and Dr. Anshu Dhar, whose invaluable assistance was crucial in completing this book.

Finally, I wish to acknowledge my mentors for their guidance and inspiration: Mr. Akshar Yadav, Padma Shree Dr. Usha Sharma, Prof. Dr. Chandrawati, Dr. Hrishikesh Pai, and Mr. Dinesh Verma and his team at Pendown Press for their professional support.

Acknowledgements

"For years, I've known Dr. Gunjan as a breath of fresh air—a true disruptor in the world of fertility and career planning. In this groundbreaking book, she shatters traditional notions, offering empowering insights and crystal-clear guidance on egg freezing and fertility preservation. A game-changer for modern women balancing ambition with family planning, this must-read guide is your roadmap to owning your future with unwavering confidence and clarity."

Dr Upasana Arora
Managing Director
Yashoda Group of Hospitals

1

To Freeze or Not to Freeze? The Classic Dilemma

Navigating the Path to Empowerment and Choice

Contemplating egg freezing, are you? I am sure there are plenty of people around you, telling you it's an unnecessary action that you are choosing.

So, stop! Hold your horses, for the moment at least before you hear me out. It's just like you never take a life insurance thinking you are going to die..... its simply to secure future of your loved ones and hopefully never needed. Similarly, by freezing your eggs you are securing your future fertility and not necessarily have to always undergo an IVF.

Egg-freezing is an option that every woman can exercise & should be encouraged to exercise because even when all is going well, life has a way of throwing curveballs at us without warning.

For instance, you could be all healthy, ready to embrace motherhood in your twenties and then boom! Something happens to damage your reproductivity and you wish you had frozen your eggs; you wish someone had told you that this was even an option. However, not every woman finds it a necessity.

If you are a modern woman navigating the complexities of your twenties to early forties, where you are juggling educational goals, career aspirations, financial independence, or perhaps still trying to balance the intricacies of a new relationship/marriage, **egg-freezing emerges as a path to freedom and stability from the pressures of surrendering to having babies by a certain age.**

It surpasses mere fertility preservation; it means taking control of your future legacy. For long, luminaries like Priyanka Chopra and other illustrious Bollywood stars have embraced this option, and now this amazing option is no longer the monopoly of celebrities. Today this option is accessible to every woman, you, me and that woman next door. But not everyone knows about it.

Sangeeta's Story of I Wish Someone Had Told Me All is Well!

Sangeeta was a happily married young woman with no care in the world. She had a loving husband, and the disagreements in her marriage were few and far between. Her in-laws were decent caring people who were supportive yet respected her privacy and individuality and she had a job that she loved.

Having been married for 2 years she was looking forward to starting a family in a year or so.

Not One, but Two Curveballs!

Unknown to her, life had other plans. At the tender age of 25, 2 years into her marriage Sangeeta unearthed a lump in her breast. She immediately consulted a doctor and after some other tests and a biopsy, **the lump was _diagnosed as cancerous._**

With support from her husband & family from both sides, she fought it bravely, but after successful cancer remission, she was in for another shock- ***due to the treatments for her cancer, her reproductive potential had evaporated, shattering her dreams of motherhood and lineage.***

It is hard to even picture her devastation in later years when she found out that an option like egg-freezing exists, an option that she could have chosen before going in for the cancer treatment.

Hindered by a lack of awareness, the prospect of egg freezing eluded her and so did her dreams of biological motherhood.

Had Sangeeta read this book in her life, her story would have definitely unfolded differently.

Angelina's Awareness & Foresight: An Example Worth Following

In stark contrast stands the valiant actress Angelina Jolie.

Jolie was faced with an alarming situation, her family history and various tests showed that she had a predisposition to breast and ovarian cancers. Jolie decided to take proactive preventive action against cancer by surgically removing both ovaries and breasts.

However, armed with awareness and foresight, ***she opted to freeze her eggs before embarking on the preventive battle against cancer.***

By safeguarding her eggs, she preserved the possibility of future motherhood saving herself any disappointment & trauma later.

So, while egg freezing is a recommended option for all women, here is a list showing the categories of women who should go in for fertility preservation & would benefit the most from egg freezing.

- **Women who want to delay childbearing for any reason:** whether waiting for the right partner, pursuing education or career goals, or looking to consolidate financially or emotionally.
- **Women who are at risk for early menopause.**
  - Having a family history of menopause below 40
  - Low levels of AMH (Anti Mullerian Hormone)
  - Low AFC (Follicles) in the ovary
- **Women who are facing fertility-damaging medical treatments for.**

- Cancer surgery or Chemotherapy
- Undergoing surgery for the prevention of cancer
- Endometriosis
- Ovarian Cysts
- Autoimmune diseases such as Rheumatoid Arthritis, Crohn's Disease etc.
- Genetic mutations (e.g. BRCA) requiring ovary removal

Do not be caught unaware— Whether confronted with ominous signs such as low AMH levels indicating diminished egg reserves or haunted by a familial legacy of premature menopause, egg freezing is your trump card, your ace in the pack, when life decides to deal you a rough hand.

For Your Notes and Queries:-

Scan this QR code and post us queries on our landing page.

2

The Downward Graph of Fertility

Flipping the Downward Fertility Spiral By Egg-Freezing

Fertility Diminishes Each Day

Aging is an undeniable and unstoppable biological progression— It comes upon you without any loud warning signals, it just keeps happening silently and stealthily from day to day, week to week, month to month and year to year.

Another undeniable biological progression is that with aging fertility takes a plunge and keeps getting less and less. Your eggs, the silent architects of new life are not resistant to aging, and bear the impact of this truth, they age as you age.

Amazing Yet Shocking Facts!

Did you know that a newborn is gifted with a lavish endowment of 1-2 million eggs?

Yet, by the advent of puberty, this huge number dwindles to a mere fraction of about 4 lakhs.

Your ovaries and the eggs inside them age as you age. As I said, fertility diminishes silently. You cannot see or feel these changes, yet they come on quicker than you think.

A woman's ability to reproduce is best between her late teens & late 20s.

As you begin to hit age 30, fertility (which means your ability to get pregnant) begins to go down. And it goes down faster once you hit your mid-30s. By 45, your fertility will reach a stage where getting pregnant naturally is unlikely if not impossible.

Age & Eggs- Inversely Proportional

You begin life with a fixed number of eggs in your ovaries and as you age, the number of eggs in your ovaries decreases. Also, as you age, the chances of developing health conditions that can affect fertility, such as fibroids and endometriosis etc. become higher.

As the curtains draw to a close at menopause, a woman is left with a meager reserve of approximately 1000 eggs which are also immature and cannot produce a baby.

Graph of age vs no of eggs

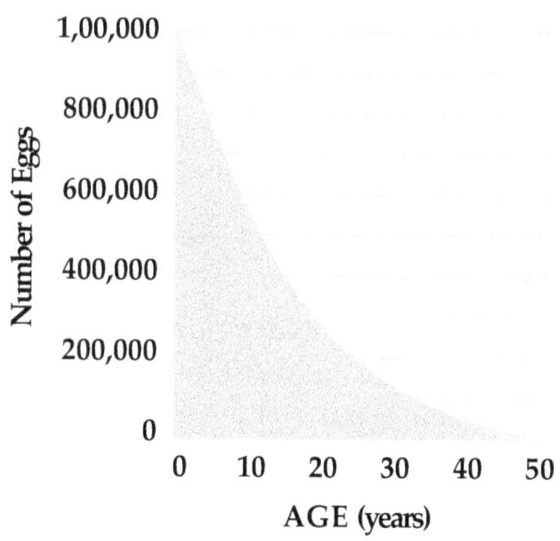

This disheartening diminishing of eggs (both in quality & numbers) is in stark contrast to the fertility of men as most of them effortlessly replenish their sperm every three months.

It's a sobering reality check, one that even the most balanced women will find themselves unprepared to confront.

This harsh reality is something that career-driven professionals, such as doctors, IT experts or bureaucrats, are blissfully unaware of at times. So caught up are they in building & advancing their careers that they do not realize the ominous non-stop ticking of the fertility clock.

The numbers don't lie.

The statistics, laid bare by the American Society of Reproductive Medicine, offer little solace.

A mere glance at the odds of natural pregnancy by age reveals a sobering reality:

Where you have a 25% chance of having a baby within the first month of trying, **it drops to 20% for women over 30 and diminishes to a daunting less than 5 % at age of 40 years—** where once there was the light of hope, now stands the dark cloud of diminishing probabilities.

For those who dare to choose the path of pregnancy beyond 40, the journey grows ever more hard, with the chances of success becoming a mere fraction of what they once were.

Busting the Myth of IVF as a Fertility Option At Later Ages

Also, here I must clear a very common misconception— that in vitro fertilization (IVF) can serve as a recourse for conceiving later in life.

However, the harsh reality is: that both natural conception and IVF using one's own eggs grow increasingly difficult with the passage of time, owing to the dwindling reserves and compromised quality of eggs.

If you want to conceive at a later age through IVF you might have to resort to using young donor eggs, which may be your only path to motherhood.

Success rates for women using young eggs— whether from a donor or from themselves, (frozen before 35)—stay stable at about 60%.

But fear not, for it's not all doom and gloom. With well-known, influential personalities like Priyanka Chopra and Diana Hayden bravely stepping into the spotlight, it is now possible for all of you to take heed of their call to action.

The time has come for collective empowerment and freedom to choose motherhood in your own time through proactive measures such as egg freezing during the bloom of your youth.

Every woman deserves the freedom to craft her life story without the burdens of fertility/infertility weighing her down.

Diana Hayden, 42, on Why She Decided to Freeze Her Eggs 8 Years Ago

She explained that the decision to freeze her eggs was an insurance of a sort - she wanted children but didn't necessarily want to get married under pressure.

"I wouldn't want to get married just to have a kid, or just to do the conventional thing. So, you give yourself that option, where there's no pressure. You hear that tick-tick behind you because you feel it,".

Diana Hayden married Collin Dick in 2013.

Diana Hayden, who agreed that Arya happened because of her foresight so many years ago, continued:

"I know how I felt when I froze my eggs. I just felt so free. Because I felt time was on my side. I can make my choices, make the right decisions and lead my life. Today, you have a choice. All you're doing is saving your chance for 'what if."

[Excerpts from an Interview given to NDTV, Jan 20, 2016]

Life-Changing Takeaways

Best Age For Egg Freezing: Your Time Starts Now

- Egg quality and quantity decrease with age. Fertility peaks between the late teens and late 20s.
- It starts declining once you reach 30 and declines sharply after 35.
- This means a woman has fewer eggs in her 40s than she does in her 20s or 30s. By 45, fertility has declined so much that

getting pregnant naturally is unlikely. Additionally, those eggs are also more likely to produce chromosomally abnormal embryos.

- As a result, our Gunjan IVF World Egg Freezing Centre team advises patients to consider freezing their eggs in their 20s or 30s. **THE SWEET SPOT IS ANYTIME BETWEEN 25 TO 34 YEARS!**
- Freezing your eggs at a younger age gives you a better chance of having a successful pregnancy and a healthy baby in the future. The younger you are the better it is.

For Your Notes and Queries:-

Scan this QR code and post us queries on our landing page.

3

Cracking The Code

Egg Quality Versus Age: A Race Against Time

Whether it be established through scientific research or often comes up in the everyday conversations of women, a stark truth emerges: **as age creeps up, so does the uncertainty of motherhood.**

Once you cross your 30s, it's like entering a new phase, where the odds start playing against you. Then imagine hitting 35, suddenly, it's like the stakes shoot up, and the risk of Down's syndrome and other complications becomes extremely high, casting a shadow over your dreams of starting a family.

Research says it loud and clear—women hit their peak fertility in their late teens to late 20s, at this time there's a surplus of healthy eggs in their ovaries.

But as the years go by, **those good eggs start vanishing, replaced by the quality-compromised, troublesome ones that make conception a tough game.**

And I don't mean just getting pregnant naturally, **even IVF cannot stop the brutal changes of genetic abnormalities that occur with increasing age in your eggs** and the chances of pregnancy drop like a stone, especially for women in their early 40s.

Now, let me explain to you the dynamics of egg, sperm and embryo— When an egg meets a sperm, it's like the egg has won a lottery and results in the formation of an embryo which leads to a pregnancy and eventually a baby.

Now here comes the twist, the real jackpot is **If you get a normal embryo meaning euploid with 46 chromosomes,** then you're golden.

But God forbid if there is even a little mess up, you end up with an **aneuploid embryo in your hands.** This means a genetically messed up embryo that is more likely to lead to a miscarriage or a baby with issues such as Down's syndrome, mental retardation and abnormal heart and other vital organs to name a few warnings of the perils that lie ahead.

From 4 abnormal embryos out of 10 in your 20s, the number peaks to a whopping 8 out of 10 at 41 and only worsens as you further age.

FERTILITY STATISTICS BY AGE

Age Brackets	Percentage of Genetically Abnormal Embryos
25-30	25%
31-35	35%
35-37	45%
38-40	60%
41-43	80%
≥44	≥80-90%

Thus it is clear that whether you are lucky enough to manage to get pregnant naturally or you go in for IVF, the fact remains that your egg quality gets compromised with age.

As a woman when you are exposed to all of the inevitable forces of everyday life—illness, toxins, free radicals, fever, and more—these damage the DNA inside your eggs.

That's why, as you grow older, **it's more likely that you'll have genetically abnormal eggs, resulting in no pregnancy, miscarriage, or genetic disorders for the baby. It's a sad but inevitable fact.**

However, there is a glimmer of light at the end of this tunnel of disappointment— Enter egg freezing—a marvel of modern medical science and technology. It is a lifeline extended to those who choose to walk the path to freedom, refusing to yield to the pressure of time & age, those who dare to defy fate and seize control of their destinies.

Life-Changing Takeaways

- As women age, the odds start stacking up against them, going from a 4 out of 10 chance of having those tricky eggs with genetic hiccups at 25, to a whopping 6 out of 10 by the time you hit 39-40 years.
- And if you're pushing past 40? Well, God help you because then it's like playing Russian roulette with your fertility—up to 8 or 9 out of 10 eggs could be problematic.
- So, if you're thinking about egg freezing, remember not just the number of eggs, but even the quality of eggs goes down drastically—the sooner you do it, the better your chances of having a healthy wholesome baby.
- Ideally, do it before you even hit 30 years. It's like an insurance policy for your future, giving you the best shot at starting a family when you're ready.

Priyanka's Words of Wisdom & Caution

Priyanka Chopra says she tells "everyone" to freeze their eggs—and to do it multiple times if possible. "I tell all ***my younger friends*** the biological clock is real," she said. ***"It gets so much harder to get pregnant after 35 and to carry to term and all of that, especially with women that have been working all their lives.***

It's the best gift you'll give yourself because you're taking the power from your biological clock, *and you can work for however long you want.* ***Your eggs will still be the same age as when you froze them."***

[On Freezing Her Eggs]

For Your Notes and Queries:-

Scan this QR code and post us queries on our landing page.

4

Evaluating Your Egg Reserve or Fertility Potential

Information is the Key to Empowerment

As a woman in your journey through life, you come to realize early on that your fertility isn't eternal. As the sands of time trickle down, you have learned from the earlier chapters that time and age are letting you down on the fertility front every passing day once you cross your 30s.

Freezing your eggs while they are still young and of good quality is your path to freedom to choose motherhood when you are ready.

Going forward in this process, it's prudent to gauge your egg reserve through an evaluation.

But the burning question in most minds is— how does one go about it?

Enter AMH (Anti-Mullerian Hormone) and AFC (Antral Follicular Count), the dynamic duo of fertility assessments.

These two fertility indicators unveil the secret stash of eggs in a woman's ovaries. All you need are fertility experts who are skilled at what they do and they can conduct these tests with ease, offering you guidance to navigate through the maze of reproductive health successfully.

So, What is AMH?

- *AMH (Anti-Mullerian Hormone) is a protein hormone secreted by specialized cells within the ovarian follicles that **holds the key to estimating our egg count.***

- A typical fertile woman boasts an AMH level ranging from 1.0 to 4.0 ng/ml; ***anything below 1.0 ng/ml signifies a diminished ovarian reserve.***
- This hormone is assessed through ***a straightforward blood test, unveiling crucial insights into reproductive health, particularly egg quantity.***
- The role of AMH is more than just numbers; it fluctuates with age and is a vital barometer of reproductive vitality. For women of childbearing age, elevated AMH levels mean a robust ovarian egg stash meaning more fertility. ***AMH gradually dwindles with advancing years until menopause, when it vanishes entirely.***

Complementing AMH is the Antral Follicle Count (AFC), which is a critical marker for fertility assessments. This simple gynecological ultrasonography unveils the number of eggs, or Antral Follicles, nestling within the ovaries.

A diminished AFC forewarns of reduced egg yield during IVF treatments, dampening the prospects of conception.

The synergy between AFC and AMH will give you a comprehensive fertility roadmap, and it can help in steering even young women towards informed choices so that they face no regrets later.

Should either of these metrics lean towards the lower spectrum, egg freezing emerges as a prudent option, safeguarding fertility for the future.

In the hands of experienced specialists, AFC and AMH will provide you with a detailed tapestry of fertility insights. Armed with this information, you feel empowered to navigate the ebbs and flows of your reproductive destiny with clarity and foresight.

Life-Changing Takeaways

- The number of eggs in the ovaries can be assessed by a dual combination of AMH and AFC.
- When these tests reveal worries, there's a ray of hope: Egg Freezing.
- It's like pressing pause on the hands of time with experienced & expert specialists who help you navigate this delicate dance between science and emotion.

For Your Notes and Queries:-

Scan this QR code and post us queries on our landing page.

5

Unveiling COVID-19's Stealth Assault on Fertility

The Pandemic Hit Fertility Too!

If things were already dark & troublesome for women's fertility post-30, they have been made worse by the COVID-19 pandemic.

Amidst the chaos of battling the immediately visible effects of the deadly COVID-19, a majority of the world seems to have overlooked the silent struggle of fertility issues.

But I speak to you with proof.

Data doesn't lie—across the globe spanning diverse nations, meticulous studies have highlighted a stark reality - **a clear link between COVID-19 and altered sex hormones, causing damage to ovarian function and fertility and eventually leading to ovarian failure.**

Guess what? I've seen it first hand in my clinic, with young girls walking in, their faces etched with worry as their menstrual cycles are all over the place.

Menstrual irregularities are just the beginning of their silent struggles, prompting investigations that reveal a disheartening truth: dwindling ovarian reserves, as evidenced by diminished AMH levels and a scant AFC (Antral Follicle count).

So, here's my message to all you young ladies—ARISE, AWAKE, AND ACT.

If your tests are showing low ovarian reserves, it's time to snap out of it. Get yourself to a fertility specialist, and seriously consider freezing your eggs for a rainy day.

It could be the smartest move you make, you will surely thank me later. Don't make the mistake of ignoring your gynecologist if they warn you of something not-so-right in your future. They only have your best interest in mind as will be evident to you from Rima's story shared below.

One Careless Decision: A Storm of Struggle—Rima's Story

There's this young power couple who waltzed into my clinic not too long ago. Rima, the wife is just 29, a go-getter in a multinational company. They'd been trying for a baby for a year. But then, bam! ***COVID hit her hard during the second wave.***

Post her recovery ***she witnessed a gradual decline in menstrual flow—a silent message of the storm brewing within.***

Incidentally, earlier on, her astute gynecologist, recognizing that she showed signs of compromised fertility had investigated ***and even warned her about her low AMH levels and advised her to freeze her eggs,*** *way before she even tied the knot.*

But guess what? ***Despite being educated and having all the info at her fingertips, she brushed it off.*** *It's human nature, we always expect that bad things always happen to somebody else and believe we are above such misfortune.*

Alas! Fast forward to a few years later, and she's now in my office, ***her AMH levels next to nil and her eggs barely visible on the ultrasound.***

It's heartbreaking to witness her tears and the desperation in her eyes as she pleads, "Doc, help me. I want my own baby, my legacy. ***Why didn't I listen to that precious advice back then?"***

Rima's story is a sobering wake-up call ladies.

Time waits for no one, and when it comes to fertility, every moment counts.

So, to **all you young women out there facing this dilemma—don't hit the snooze button. Take action now, before it's too late.** Your future self will thank you for it

May Rima's tale serve as a strong reminder—a testimonial to the undeniable truth that time, once lost, can never be reclaimed.

Today, within your grasp lies the power to shape your destiny—to take the decision of creating a new life when you choose instead of time deciding it for you by default.

Life-Changing Takeaways

- If you have suffered Covid 19 and are having menstrual irregularities, you must get yourself a fertility assessment as soon as possible.
- On the other hand, even if you are just curious to get yourself evaluated for ovarian reserves, go for it! Get yourself tested.
- In both cases, if you get a clean bill of health, it will put your mind at ease, but if things look concerning, you can immediately consider egg freezing as a backup plan. Trust me, a little peace of mind goes a long way.

For Your Notes and Queries:-

Scan this QR code and post us queries on our landing page.

6

6 Steps to Fertility Freedom

A Clear Roadmap to Navigating Fertility

Now that you completely understand the importance of freezing your eggs and also the heart-breaking consequences of not doing so, I am sure the question that is topmost in your mind right now is how do we go about it?

Let me put your mind at rest, for in this chapter I am giving you a clear and complete roadmap to fertility freedom step-by-step.

Step 1— A Fertility Check-Up

Alright, ladies, your journey to fertility freedom kicks off with a fertility assessment.

A fertility assessment would typically be a 30 to 45-minute session where the respective experts and clinicians would dive deep into your reproductive health using a transvaginal ultrasound and a simple blood test. This would help them figure out your ovarian reserve, in simple words, the number of eggs in your ovaries.

Step 2— Meeting Your Fertility Specialist

After the diagnostic assessment comes your doctor's appointment. This is where you sit down with your friendly fertility specialist. In this session, together with your fertility specialist, you'll chat about your medical history and go over the assessment results received in the first step that we talked about above.

Also, this session is where your fertility expert will explain to you about egg freezing in detail. **In fact, a great fertility specialist will explain it all so well to you that it'll be like a crash course**

in egg freezing - the science, the process, and what you can expect.

Oh, and don't forget, your doctor will also map out a stimulation plan to make sure that you get as many eggs as possible safely.

Step 3: Pump it Up!: The Stimulation Process

Once you've committed to your freedom by deciding to freeze your eggs, your doctor will put you on a stimulation plan to get those ovaries fired up! **This means that you'll be taking hormone injections for about 8 to 12 days to stimulate those ovaries into egg-making overdrive.**

While this process is going on, your fertility expert will keep a close eye on the proceedings with ultrasounds and blood tests to make sure everything's on track.

Step 4: The Egg Hunt!

Now comes the exciting part - the egg retrieval!

This is a quick surgical procedure, about 15 to 30 minutes at the most, where your precious eggs are carefully and safely plucked out of your ovaries.

And before you become anxious about this procedure, I'd like to reassure you that there is nothing to worry about. You'll be snoozing through the whole thing thanks to some deep sedation. **Also, this is a minimally invasive procedure— No cuts, no stitches, just a little needle action through the vaginal wall and you are sorted. Easy peasy!**

Step 5: Freeze 'Em Up

Once your specialist has nabbed your eggs, it's time to freeze them!

Ok, now I want you to be clear that this is not your ordinary freezing-in-a-freezer that we are talking about. **The process of freezing your eggs is called vitrification - which means flash-freezing your eggs in liquid nitrogen.** This minimizes the risk of ice crystal formation and ensures your eggs stay nice and cozy until you're ready to use them.

Step 6: Recovery Mode

Alright, you've made it through the hard part, now it's time to sit back and relax. **You might experience a bit of cramping, bloating, or spotting in the first 24 hours, but nothing a heating pad and some over-the-counter pain meds can't handle.** But hey, if things get rough, don't hesitate to reach out to your doctor.

The majority, of women are back on their feet and ready to tackle the world the next day!

So, there you have it, ladies - six simple steps to your fertility freedom!

With these six simple steps, you can take control of your reproductive future and make those dreams of motherhood come true at a time of choice irrespective of your age.

Life-Changing Takeaways

- The process of egg freezing involves 6 simple steps spread out approximately over 2 weeks which help you to get your eggs frozen for the future.

- The process of egg retrieval is a short-day care procedure and does not involve any cuts, is not painful and you are not required to be off work for more than a day

For Your Notes and Queries:-

Scan this QR code and post us queries on our landing page.

7

Eggs–actly How Many Should You Freeze

Decoding the Numbers Game

"If you're pondering 'How Many Eggs Should I Freeze?' - You are not alone, once you've understood the process and committed to the decision— How many eggs to freeze is the million Rupee question that immediately comes to mind.

Determining how many eggs to freeze is like drafting a blueprint for your future family, and it's a question I often get asked. Here's the thing: it's not a one-size-fits-all answer. It's like trying to solve a complex equation where the variables keep changing.

This question is definitely not a simple one to answer as there are many facets to consider, however, a great fertility specialist will be able to help you answer this satisfactorily.

Here I am sharing with you the **Key Factors** to consider to decide how many eggs to freeze.

First off, you need to consider how many little ones you want running around in the future. Do you see yourself with just one bundle of joy or do you envision a bigger family?

Your answer to this will give you a ballpark figure of how many eggs you might need to freeze.

Next up, age plays a significant role. It's like the ticking of a clock in the background. The younger you are when you freeze your eggs, the better the quality and quantity you're likely to get.

As time ticks on, your egg quality can take a hit, so you might need to freeze more eggs as insurance bets against Mother Nature.

Then there's the yield from each egg retrieval cycle.

Think of it like going on a treasure hunt. Sometimes you strike gold, sometimes you come back empty-handed.

The number of eggs retrieved can vary from cycle to cycle, depending on your body's response.

Now, let's talk about success rates. It's like trying to predict the weather – there are no guarantees. **Success rates with egg freezing and pregnancy vary with age. The older you are, the more eggs you might need to freeze to increase your chances of a successful pregnancy down the line.**

So, how many eggs should you freeze?

The ballpark figure is around 10-15 eggs per planned pregnancy attempt, but remember, this isn't set in stone.

It's like aiming for a target on a moving train – you need to adjust your aim as you go along. Factors like sperm quality, egg quality, and age all come into play, influencing the final outcome.

In the end, it's a decision best made in consultation with a fertility specialist. They're like your navigators in this journey, guiding you through the maze of options and helping you make the best decision for your future family.

So, let's look at all these factors in detail.

Factor #1

Your age is crucial in determining the number of eggs you should freeze.

As you age, the DNA in your eggs is more likely to have abnormalities, leading to a decline in egg quality.

Consequently, **older women are advised to freeze more eggs compared to younger women to achieve a similar level of confidence in successful pregnancies.**

Research done on 520 women from Brigham and women in Boston suggests that women under 35 who freeze 10–20 eggs have a 70-90% chance of at least one live birth later on.

However, this chance decreases with age due to declining egg quality.

If a 38-year-old freezes the same 15 eggs, that would represent only a 60% chance of having a baby. So, a 38-year-old woman may need to freeze 30 or more eggs to have the same 85% chance of having a baby as a younger woman with 15 frozen eggs.

The optimal outcome is to freeze enough eggs to attain an estimated 70% chance of a live birth from these eggs in the future.

This optimal number varies based on age, as shown in the table below:

Age Bracket	**Number of Eggs for a 50% Live Birth Rate**	**Number of Eggs for a 60% Live Birth Rate**	**Number of Eggs for a 70% Live Birth Rate**
<35	6	8	9
35-37	7	8	10
38-41	11	13	16

41-42	20	24	28
>42	50	70	80

It's important to consider your age and the level of success you're comfortable with when deciding how many eggs to freeze.

Factor 1.1

Also important is your Age = how many eggs you might freeze in each cycle

So the other question you should be asking, is how many cycles you might need to get to that number. This, too, is usually based on your age.

> ***Ovarian reserve testing helps estimate the number of eggs you might produce per cycle, which influences the number of cycles needed to reach your egg-freezing goal.***

Younger women tend to produce more eggs per cycle and may need fewer cycles, while older women may produce fewer eggs per cycle and require more cycles to reach their goal.

Therefore, it's advisable for women to **consider egg freezing in their late 20s or early 30s to maximize the chances of success per egg** and reduce the need for multiple cycles.

Factor #2

Your family goals

Family goals are a crucial consideration when determining how many eggs you should freeze. Your desired family size—whether it's one child, three children, or simply preserving the option for future use—affects the recommendation for egg freezing.

Key Points:

- **Family Size:** If you envision a larger family, you'll need a more substantial reserve of frozen eggs for each additional child. The factors influencing success for the first child also apply to subsequent children.
- **Success Probability:** The number of eggs you freeze influences the likelihood of achieving your desired family size. **For instance, a 30-year-old woman with 15 frozen eggs has an 83% chance of one birth, a 50% chance of two, and only a 22% chance of three.** Therefore, if you aspire to have a larger family, freezing more eggs enhances the probability of multiple children.
- **Natural Conception:** It's essential to acknowledge the possibility of natural conception for the first child, which may reduce the immediate need to use frozen eggs. Nonetheless, if your goal is multiple children, freezing additional eggs provides future options.

In summary, understanding your family goals is paramount in determining the optimal number of eggs to freeze, ensuring greater flexibility and success in achieving your desired family size.

Factor #3

Your budget and time: A crucial aspect to ponder

Deciding how many eggs to freeze may not be the most enjoyable topic, as it involves finances too. Therefore financial constraints many a times also influence this decision for many women.

Key Points:

- **Financial Considerations:** The cost of egg freezing can be a significant factor in determining the number of cycles you can afford. **Assessing your budget realistically is essential to determine how many cycles you can undergo.**

- **Affordability:** Since my mission is to make egg freezing accessible to as many women as possible, my team and I at Gunjan IVF World have made special efforts to make egg freezing more accessible by lowering costs and offering convenient payment options. **By making the process more affordable, more women can pursue their egg-freezing goals within their financial means.**

- **Role of the Fertility Clinic:** Your fertility doctor and clinic play a crucial role in guiding you through the process. They can provide insights into costs, help you understand available options, and support you in making decisions aligned with your budget and goals.

In summary, understanding your financial situation and the affordability of egg freezing is vital in deciding how many eggs to freeze. While it involves an investment, efforts to make it more accessible are ongoing and your fertility clinic can provide valuable assistance throughout the process.

Life-Changing Takeaways

- Determining the number of eggs to freeze is a complex decision influenced by various factors. Here's a breakdown of the key considerations:

- **Desired Number of Children:** The number of eggs you freeze may depend on how many children you wish to have in the future. If you plan to have multiple children, you may need to freeze a larger number of eggs.

- **Age at the Time of Egg Freezing:** Your age at the time of egg freezing is crucial. Generally, younger individuals tend to produce more viable eggs. As you age, the quality and quantity of your eggs may decline, necessitating the freezing of more eggs for future use.
- **Egg Retrieval Yield:** The number of eggs retrieved in one cycle of egg freezing can vary. Factors such as ovarian reserve and response to ovarian stimulation can influence the number of eggs obtained.
- **Success Rates and Age:** Success rates for egg freezing and subsequent pregnancy vary with age. Older individuals may require a higher number of eggs to achieve successful pregnancy outcomes due to decreased egg quality and lower implantation rates.
- **Considering these factors, it's recommended to freeze at least 10-15 eggs per planned pregnancy attempt,** but this number may need adjustment based on individual circumstances and age. Consulting with a fertility specialist is crucial to determine the optimal number of eggs to freeze for your specific situation.
- **The younger, the better**— Fewer eggs are required to achieve the target of having a baby despite a higher number being available at younger age as the quality of eggs is better.

❍ ❍ ❍ ❍

For Your Notes and Queries:-

Scan this QR code and post us queries on our landing page.

8

13 Egg-cellent Considerations Choosing Your Egg Freezing Guru

Hey, ladies! So, you're thinking about freezing your eggs? Big step huh?

But before you jump in, you gotta know what you're getting into. Your eggs, & your future is all at stake.

The whole process of egg freezing is such a delicate interplay of science, emotions, information, expertise and trust that it needs to be handled with the utmost care & consideration.

What can truly make the process smooth and anxiety-free is the partnership between you and your fertility expert!

Here are 12 key things you need to look for in your egg-freezing specialist. Trust me, it's worth it."

1. **Is the clinic registered as per the ART law, 2022, India?**
   - Choose registered IVF clinics only
2. **What does the grapevine say about this clinic? Reputation matters, you know.**
   - Do some online stalking, check Google reviews, Instagram, Facebook - the whole spectrum of social Media. But don't fall for just one review, dig deeper to see the overall trend. You can even ask friends and family who are nearby to the clinic to check it out and get feedback from the neighbourhood.
3. **Who are the people running the show? Are the doctors and embryologists qualified or just winging it?**

- Look for the team, the IVF Centre offers. Prefer centres that have a team of multiple, trained and qualified IVF specialists and Embryologists supported by other fertility professionals, nurses and a support team of counsellors and relationship managers.

4. **What's the technology capability & status of the establishment? Are they freezing eggs with cutting-edge state-of-the-art technology or are they stuck with outdated technology?**
   - It's important to understand the method of cryopreservation (freezing) the laboratory uses: The two methods are slow freezing, which is the older, less effective method; **and vitrification, the new method that has made egg freezing an effective treatment.**
   - All egg-freezing practices should be using vitrification, as egg survival rates (the percentage of eggs that are still viable after being frozen and thawed) for vitrification are around 90% (compared to around 60% for slow freezing).
   - If your potential provider is using slow freezing, it's a no-go. You should choose a clinic using the vitrification technique. Here at Gunjan IVF World, **we use an advanced vitrification protocol designed to ensure the highest possible success rates for frozen eggs.**
   - The type of incubator used in the lab also matters. Incubators are used in the lab to keep eggs at the ideal temperature and pH until they're frozen. At some labs, they use a large "box incubator" that contains many patients' eggs. The problem with a box incubator is that every time the incubator is opened to access a patient's

eggs, the environment inside changes—and because box incubators are larger, it takes longer for their interiors to return to the optimal temperature and pH.

- **A superior piece of equipment is a benchtop incubator** like we use in our lab. The six small chambers of the benchtop incubator each contain only one patient's eggs, allowing precise control and stability of the incubator environment.

5. **Where are my precious eggs going to chill? On-site storage or some shady warehouse?**
   - In India, it is preferable to have centres which have on-site storage facilities which means freezing should be done at the same place where the picking or retrieval of eggs has been done.

6. **What's the game plan if I decide to use these eggs? Paint me a picture of the process.**
   - In the future, when the time comes for you to use your eggs, the frozen eggs must be thawed (de-freeze) in a lab and fertilized in a process known as in vitro fertilization or IVF, which creates embryos that can then be transferred back into your uterus.
   - While many women freeze their eggs in the hope that they'll never need to use them, it's important to understand what will happen if you do.

7. **Can I use my eggs here in future at the same fertility clinic?**
   - We here at Gunjan IVF World offer our patients a seamless and affordable experience when using their eggs (in addition to offering affordable full-service fertility care).

8. **What's the deal if I decide to relocate? Will the clinic still support me or will they make it a hassle? Do they have any policy on it?**
    - If you move or want to use your eggs with another facility for any reason (like, say, you move to another city) It's important that your provider offers an easy option to transfer your eggs to another laboratory, and can communicate lab protocols to allow for the optimal thawing of your eggs.
9. **Don't forget to check the Fertility Clinic's scorecard. At the end of the day, success rates matter, darling!**
    - IVF Centres with higher success rates will have better SOPs even for egg freezing and hence better results for you. It is safe to say how they do one thing is how they do everything.
10. **What are the price tags? Money matters, but don't get blinded by the digits, #Quality over discounts, always.......**
    - It's important that you understand what that cycle price includes.
    - Ask the Centre about the charges for freezing and the annual renewal policy.
    - Does it cover the cost of your consultations during the procedure, or is that a separate charge?
    - Is anaesthesia for the egg retrieval included?
    - Is additional required testing included?
    - Make sure you fully understand the breakdown of what you're paying, so you can accurately compare providers—and avoid any surprise bills later.

However, I would like to add a disclaimer, pricing should not be your only important consideration as the eggs have to be stored for a long time, so the reputation, technique and technology used by the Clinic are very important

11. **Do they have insurance for when Mother Nature decides to throw a tantrum?**
    - It is very important for you to know if the Clinic has insurance in case of natural calamities, such as earthquakes, fire, floods etc.
12. **Do you vibe with the crew? Your trust & comfort level with the team will make all the difference to your experience.**
    - Make sure to choose a centre where you are comfortable and they give you personalised care.

Confidentiality & Privacy— The Two Cornerstones of The Right Fertility Partner

The last yet most important question is this— Can you expect complete confidentiality and privacy from your fertility specialist and their clinic?

Since egg freezing is a deeply personal choice, you may or may not be comfortable with sharing that information with everyone. For some people, this might be such a sensitive concern that they may hesitate or even choose not to freeze their eggs for the fear of it becoming a subject of public discussion or media scrutiny.

Here at Gunjan IVF World, we have helped many such people.

Let me share with you the story of a power couple who were well-known in the political domain. It is a known fact that the lives of people serving the nation through politics are laid bare for everyone to see. All their private details are scrutinised, discussed and judged. So was the case with this couple.

They wanted to freeze the wife's eggs to use later when they both felt ready to be parents. However, due to the media spotlight on them, they were hesitant and unwilling to trust any specialist or clinic.

They feared that somebody on the team at the clinic they chose would leak their decision to the press/online.

A couple of years passed in this dilemma and they thought they would never be able to make this a reality. One day, the husband happened to meet me at an international event where we were both speaking.

After the event, he spoke to me privately about their desire to freeze the wife's eggs. I told him that it was a great idea and then he voiced his concern about their decision turning into a media circus.

I immediately set all his doubts at rest by explaining to him our core value policy of offering the utmost privacy & confidentiality to our clients.

I informed him that we had a ***complete software system for masking the client's real names in all our communication to the extent that until the person walked in, our staff even did not know that a highly visible or well-known client would be coming in.***

I also explained to him how ***our entire team in all departments top to bottom is sensitised, trained and counselled about maintaining confidentiality at the highest level.***

Placing faith in us the couple finally did manage to freeze the wife's eggs and to date, no one knows a word about this.

They always keep thanking me profusely even today. ***This sensitivity towards a client's need for confidentiality and the system to ensure it has helped us serve many high-profile & visible clients.***

Life-Changing Takeaways

- Before choosing an egg-freezing partner check for a place which has a good reputation and is known for using advanced cutting-edge technology, operates transparently, has a track record of successful results, can offer you complete confidentiality and gives you value for your effort and money.

For Your Notes and Queries:-

Scan this QR code and post us queries on our landing page.

9

Don't Get Caught in The Trap of Baseless Negativity

Busting Myths About Egg-Freezing

Despite the growing popularity and success of egg freezing, several misconceptions still prevent many individuals from considering this beneficial reproductive option of choice.

These myths generate unnecessary fears and misunderstandings, preventing people from exploring a procedure that could greatly enhance their reproductive choices and flexibility.

That is why I am dispelling these myths here by dedicating an entire section to them, to provide women (and couples)clarity and to encourage more informed decisions regarding egg freezing.

So let's start shooting those myths down right away—

Myth #1: Egg Freezing Uses Up All Your Eggs

Fact: Egg freezing does not deplete your natural egg reserve. The process involves harvesting eggs that would have otherwise been naturally absorbed by your body. Thus, it does not reduce your overall egg count or affect your future fertility.

Myth #2: Egg Freezing is a Complicated Procedure

Fact: The process of egg freezing is relatively straightforward, involving a few key steps that I've already detailed in Chapter 6, recapping briefly here again:

- **Ovarian Stimulation:** Hormonal medications are used to increase the number of available eggs for retrieval.
- **Monitoring:** The growth and maturity of the eggs are assessed.

- **Egg Retrieval:** A brief, minimally invasive procedure performed under anesthesia to collect mature eggs.
- **Cryopreservation:** The eggs are tested for quality and then frozen through vitrification, which involves cryoprotectants and rapid cooling.
- **Storage:** The eggs are kept at very low temperatures until they are thawed for in-vitro fertilization (IVF).

Myth #3: Egg Freezing Can Harm Natural Fertility

Fact: The belief that egg freezing reduces the natural supply of viable eggs is a misconception. While individuals are born with a finite number of eggs, many are naturally lost over time. Ovarian stimulation, a critical part of egg freezing, encourages more than one eggs to mature simultaneously without depleting the natural reserve. **This process preserves additional eggs for future use, leaving natural fertility unaffected.**

Myth #4: EGG freezing means 100% IVF is required:

Fact: Egg freezing is just an Insurance to secure future fertility, in case you have a problem in conceiving naturally in future these eggs can be utilized giving you the best chance of having a baby especially if frozen at the right age. Even after freezing your eggs you can try and have a baby naturally SO IN ALL CASES IVF IS NOT REQUIRED

Myth #5: Egg Freezing is Unsafe

Fact: Egg freezing is generally safe, though there are some risks and side effects, mainly from the hormonal medications used in ovarian stimulation. Most side effects are mild, such as bloating and discomfort, similar to those experienced during a menstrual cycle. Rarely, severe complications like ovarian hyperstimulation syndrome (OHSS) can occur, but close monitoring by healthcare professionals ensures safety throughout the procedure.

Myth #6:Egg freezing and embryo freezing are the same

Fact: Egg freezing and embryo freezing largely involve the same steps for the individual undergoing the procedure. However, with embryo freezing you are going through the process of fertilizing the egg in the lab with sperm. You then will have the embryos frozen at the end of 5-7 days of growth in the lab. One of the biggest differences between egg and embryo freezing is the concept of reproductive autonomy. In short, freezing eggs gives you the opportunity to defer into the future the decision about where the sperm will come from. Furthermore, there are some legal pitfalls to be aware of when an embryo is frozen vs when eggs are frozen.

A Disclaimer

Myth #7: Egg freezing guarantees you'll be able to have a successful pregnancy later in life.

Facts: Fertility, conception, pregnancy, and birth are all exceptionally complex processes. While egg freezing can markedly improve your chances of conceiving later in life, it is not a guarantee. Many factors are at play when it comes to having a successful conception and pregnancy, with eggs being only one aspect.

For Your Notes and Queries:-

Scan this QR code and post us queries on our landing page.

10

You Ask [FAQs]: India's #1 Fertility Specialist Answers

Dr. Gunjan Gupta Shows You How to Freeze It Right

1. "How Long Can My Eggs Hang in the Freezer?"

You know, there's no set limit to how long your eggs can chill in the freezer. It's kind of incredible, but the longest thaw recorded has been a whopping 14 years! And get this, loads of healthy babies have come into the world from eggs frozen for like 5 to 10 years. Once they're frozen, those little guys are kept safe and sound in a super secure facility until you're good to go. For eggs to be stored indefinitely it is unknown if there is deterioration over time in storage. So, whenever you're ready, just thaw them out, and voila, you're on your way to parenthood!

2. Does Egg Freezing Mess with Future Fertility or Hurt Future Pregnancy Chances?"

While considering the prospect of freezing eggs, many women wonder about its impact on fertility. **The reassuring truth is that freezing eggs does not impede fertility.** Your ovarian reserve, which denotes the number of viable eggs, generally remains unaffected by the process.

To understand this better, let's delve briefly into the ovulation mechanism. Monthly, only one egg usually survives the journey to ovulation. Although multiple follicles are initiated, only one egg typically matures fully, while the rest undergo a natural process known as "atresia" and are naturally discarded.

Dr. Gunjan Gupta says that egg freezing essentially preserves some of these eggs that would otherwise perish.

During the egg-freezing procedure, hormonal medications prompt the ovaries to produce multiple mature eggs in a cycle, as opposed to the usual single egg that would mature naturally. Subsequently, these eggs are harvested and preserved for potential future use.

Consequently, egg freezing does not deplete your ovarian reserve, nor does it jeopardize your prospects of conceiving naturally later on. Rather, the frozen eggs serve as a contingency plan should you encounter challenges with conception when you decide to start a family in the future.

3. Do Frozen Eggs Lead to any Baby Risks?

Alright, folks, let's talk about frozen eggs and the risks to the little ones. You might be worried, thinking, 'Hey, could there be any problems for my baby if I go this route?' Well, here's the news: **there's no evidence to suggest that kids conceived with frozen eggs have more chromosomal quirks, birth defects, or developmental hiccups. None, not at all.**

In fact, using top-notch frozen eggs, especially ones scooped up when you're younger, can actually dial down the risks linked with being an older mom. You know, stuff like having a higher chance of miscarriage or genetically abnormal babies etc...

So, if you're a lady in your forties or beyond, listen up. You might just have a better shot at a smooth-sailing pregnancy using those frozen eggs you grabbed back when you were younger & the quality of your eggs was premium in your early- mid-thirties.

4. What Are The Side Effects of Egg Freezing: Here's Everything You Need to Know!

Now, let's talk real talk about the medical stuff. Here, I am going to be completely honest with you.

Like any medical procedure, egg freezing comes with its own set of possible side effects – no getting around it. You might feel a bit like you're riding the monthly hormone rollercoaster, with tiredness, mood swings, and tender breasts thanks to the medication. Plus, you might notice some soreness or redness at the site of the injections.

After the egg retrieval, some women might experience a bit of discomfort down the pelvis or vagina, but nothing a couple of paracetamols can't handle. Most ladies are back to business as usual at work the next day.

Sure, in rare cases, your ovaries might decide to go into overdrive from all those hormones (it's called 'ovarian hyperstimulation syndrome'). But don't sweat it too much – a top-notch fertility clinic will keep a close eye on you, making sure you're sailing smoothly by adjusting your meds as needed. So, while there may be a few bumps on the road, there's no major cause for worry, it's usually smooth sailing.

Mona Singh On Her Egg-freezing Journey

&

Keeping The Eye On The Goal

Famed television & movie actress Mona Singh was one of the first celebrities who talked about her egg-freezing journey out loud.

She said, "Our family gynecologist came over for dinner with his wife and told my parents and me that you should think of freezing your eggs. Because yes, the clock is ticking, and even if you don't want to get married in the next five years, at least you have this. You have frozen your eggs and whenever you want to have a baby, you can always rely on that. So, I was like okay! This kind of makes sense."

Elaborating further about the experience and the time it took, Mona added, "About 3 to 6 months and maybe sometimes it can be a bit painful because you will go through a lot of mood swings. Your body will change. A little bit of hormones being injected. You will bloat some days. Some days, you will not feel good about yourself. ***But it's only 3 to 6 months. You do it once and then you forget about it. And then get married whenever you want to, no pressure!***

At least you're not marrying the wrong guy for a baby.

5. Is it possible to freeze my eggs if I'm aged 40 or above?

Yes, it is possible to freeze eggs later in life; however, as the number of eggs produced by the body decreases with age, the quantity of eggs available for extraction and freezing will be limited. Pregnancy success rates are lower for eggs frozen after the age of 35, so it is typically recommended to undergo egg freezing at a younger age.

For women over forty who wish to postpone fertility, using donated eggs from a younger woman is often advised.

6. How many eggs can be frozen?

To give a woman a reasonable chance of having a live birth, approximately 30-40 eggs need to be stored. This often requires undergoing at least 2-5 treatment cycles to ensure that a sufficient number of mature eggs are collected. It's important to note that having a large number of eggs stored does not guarantee a live birth.

7. Is egg-freezing legal in India?

Yes, egg-freezing is allowed in India. There is no specific law governing this,but it falls under the purview of the Assisted Reproductive Technologies (Regulation)Act [ART], 2021.

For Your Notes and Queries:-

Scan this QR code and post us queries on our landing page.

11

Prepping For Egg-Freezing Bonus Tips To Make The Journey Smoother

Embarking on the journey of egg freezing requires careful preparation and consideration across multiple aspects of life. In this chapter I am sharing with you additional comprehensive guidance on how to navigate the financial, emotional, and logistical aspects of the process, to ensure you are well-prepared and supported throughout.

Visit Our Landing page On all nitty-gritties on EGG Freezing. It will help you get ready..................

Financial Considerations

Though worth its weight in gold or I'd say invaluable, egg freezing can be a significant financial investment. It's crucial to evaluate your budget, explore various financial avenues as per your situation and plan accordingly.

Investigate insurance policies to see if they cover any part of the procedure, check with your employer for possible benefits, and research & consider if financing programs are available for fertility treatments. Taking these steps can help make the process more stress-free and manageable.

Emotional Preparedness

While a great fertility specialist will hold your hand gently & caringly all the way through, the journey of egg-freezing can be emotionally delicate. It's essential to acknowledge this and seek the necessary emotional support. Lean on friends and family who can offer a listening ear and encouragement. Additionally, you could consider speaking with a counsellor who specializes in fertility issues to help navigate the emotional landscape of this experience.

Time Commitment and Management

Understanding the time commitment involved in egg-freezing is crucial for effective planning. The process includes a medication regimen, frequent monitoring appointments, and the egg retrieval procedure itself. Organize your schedule to accommodate these commitments, and plan ahead to minimize stress and disruptions to your daily life.

Health and Wellness

Maintaining a healthy lifestyle is vital during the egg-freezing process. Regular physical activity, a nutritious diet, and effective stress management can all positively influence your fertility and the success of the procedure. Prioritize your overall well-being to optimize your body's readiness for egg retrieval and preservation.

Setting Realistic Expectations

While egg freezing can increase the likelihood of future pregnancy, it is not a definitive guarantee. It's important to manage your expectations and understand that individual results can vary. Being realistic about the potential outcomes will help you navigate the process with a balanced perspective.

Seeking Support Groups

Humans thrive on social validation and communities with common grounds can be a powerful support tool. Connecting with others who are undergoing similar experiences can provide invaluable support and advice. Join support groups or online communities where you can share stories, gather insights, and receive encouragement.

Although effective India-based groups might be scarce, there are numerous international communities available. These groups discuss practicalities, share experiences, and offer a sense of solidarity, helping you feel less isolated in your journey.

By addressing these aspects of financial planning, emotional support, time management, health, and realistic expectations, you can better prepare for the egg-freezing process and increase your chances of a successful outcome.

For Your Notes and Queries:-

Scan this QR code and post us queries on our landing page.

Your Path to Freedom and Empowerment

"Take control of your life with egg freezing under the expert guidance of Dr. Gunjan Gupta Govil and her experienced team at Gunjan IVF World. Don't let the biological clock limit your dreams—secure your future today. Book a discovery appointment and take the first step toward informed and empowered choices. For more insights and updates, stay connected with Gunjan IVF World through our social media channels."As a woman how many times have you heard these questions:

https://www.linkedin.com/company/gunjan-ivf-world/

https://youtube.com/gunjanivfworld

https://www.facebook.com/GunjanIVFWorld/

https://www.instagram.com/gunjanivfworld/

❍ ❍ ❍ ❍

www.ingramcontent.com/pod-product-compliance
Ingram Content Group UK Ltd.
Pitfield, Milton Keynes, MK11 3LW, UK
UKHW021656190726
13853UKWH00001B/291